Just ME, *Lucy*, AND THE LORD

A 31-DAY DEVOTIONAL

DON HOCKER

HIGH BRIDGE BOOKS
HOUSTON

Just Me, Lucy, and the Lord
by Don Hocker

Copyright © 2021 by Don Hocker

All rights reserved.

Printed in the United States of America
ISBN: 978-1-954943-29-2

All Scripture quotations marked NIV are taken from THE HOLY BIBLE, NEW INTERNATIONAL VERSION®, NIV® Copyright © 1973, 1978, 1984, 2011 by Biblica, Inc.® Used by permission. All rights reserved worldwide.

High Bridge Books titles may be purchased in bulk for educational, business, fundraising, or sales promotional use. For information, please contact High Bridge Books via www.HighBridgeBooks.com/contact.

Published in Houston, Texas by High Bridge Books

This devotional book is dedicated to my wonderful family:
wife, Gayle; son, Mike; daughter, Kathryn;
daughter-in-law, Mandy; and grandson, Ford.

CONTENTS

INTRODUCTION

I WAS SAVED ON FEBRUARY 15, 2011, AND MORE ABOUT THAT DAY in a minute. Let me go back in time and put things in context. I grew up in the church. It was rare that we would miss a Sunday. After getting married and having children, it was business as usual. We were in church. Like many people, I have held leadership positions in church and served on just about every committee there was. I even taught Sunday School, which I still do today.

I thought I had it together and certainly could call myself a Christian. But the sad thing was I never picked up the Bible except to prepare for a Sunday School lesson, but still, that was really just a formality. My prayer life? Whew! Not much of one unless it was one of those times when we say, "Oh God, I need your help!" So for years, I thought it was plenty enough to be able to say, "Sure, I know about God, and I know that Jesus died on the cross."

Then, God started working on me. In September 2010, I started attending a men's Tuesday lunch Bible study. In November of 2010, my family bought, at my request, a really nice Bible, and it was a genuine leather bible, and it was in the King James translation. Now I was very grateful for this gift, but when you are a novice at reading scripture, Yikes! This translation, however very much respected and revered, makes it a little difficult.

Anyways, I started every morning around this same time with this King James Bible in hand, reading and trying to understand scripture. Also, it is worthy of mentioning that Gayle and I did a five-week couple's Bible study, creatively and fondly called Couple's Boot Camp, in January 2011. So my routine was this. I would fix breakfast for Gayle and myself, as both kids were out of the home, and would clean up as Gayle was finishing up getting ready to go to work. Out the door she went, and it was then just me and our beloved dachshund, Lucy. I would always have my "quiet time" in the mornings before I went to work. Starting out, I would pick up Lucy and carry her to my study so she could sit with me. She loved to snuggle in a chair with the family.

One morning, after a few mornings of doing this, and it was time for my "quiet time," I walked past Lucy where she would always be in her bed under a built-in desk in the kitchen, and I did not pick her up. I was headed toward the study, and I kid you not, she knew what I was going to do. So she got up out of her bed and followed me to the study. From that point forward every morning until her death about three years later, I never had to say a word. When I finished in the kitchen and walked past her to the study, here she would be walking behind me for me to put her in my chair, and she would sit with me for as long as I was there. It was just me, Lucy, and the Lord!

So, the morning of February 15, 2011, was historical for me. I came to the realization that I could not do life by myself. I finally knew that I needed God with me and that he loved me so much that he allowed his most precious Son to die for me. I got on my knees with Lucy in the chair, and I cried. God humbled me that morning, and for that I am so very grateful! I just simply came to the conclusion that I needed God in charge of my life, that I needed Jesus as my Savior, and I needed the Holy Spirit to guide and direct me through all the twists and turns of what we call life.

Several years ago, God tapped me on the shoulder and said, "Be thinking about writing a book about your faith and maybe throw in some experiences along with it." I was not too crazy about the idea—never thought I was much of a writer. Sure, I penned[1] out a few things along the way. But a book? Never crossed my mind. Never a thought. Never a desire. Never a clue that I would personally dive into the unchartered waters of being an author. And also, don't writers have to be somewhat creative? No creative bone in this body. I am pretty much a meat and potatoes guy. So I dismissed the idea.

Well, along came another tap. God can be pretty persistent sometimes, and I have come to learn that he is persistent because He cares. He truly does. So, I started a book with a title for the book, wrote an introduction and about two and a half chapters, and then I got writer's block. Hit a brick wall. I couldn't go any further.

I think my problem was that I did not have a vision for the book—not even an outline. I had no direction, and sadly enough, I did not ask God for any help. So the partial manuscript was shelved away without much more thought.

Several years later, another tap on my shoulder. God laid it on my heart to write a devotional book. I didn't really need an outline. Just select various passages in scripture that have meaning to me, that I like a lot, and that I can discuss with a sprinkling of my faith that I have developed over these few years. So I decided to dive in and give it a go.

A disclaimer: I am not an expert theologian. I am not a Bible scholar. You will not hear me say: "The Greek word for … The Hebrew word for …" I do not know any Greek or Hebrew, okay? I am just a novice Christian who loves the Lord. These devotionals simply contain my simple understanding of what the various scripture passages mean to me.

If this modest devotional book touches one person in a special way, then I will be forever grateful and truly humbled.

---

[1] Alright, any of you youngins daring enough to read this book: "Penned" means to use a pen or pencil to write words by hand.

Day One

CREATION

"For in him all things were created: things in heaven and on earth, visible and invisible, whether thrones or powers or rulers or authorities; all things have been created through him and for him."

—Colossians 1:16 NIV

DID YOU KNOW THAT MOUNT EVEREST HAS AN ELEVATION OF 29,029 feet?

Did you know the human brain contains 100,000 miles of blood vessels and can process information up to a speed of 268 miles per hour?[1]

Did you know a tiny hummingbird has wings that beat 200 times a second when diving?[2]

My wife, Gayle, and I had the opportunity to travel with friends several years ago to the Grand Canyon and other spectacular places in Arizona and Utah. What an amazing work of creation. Gayle and I both said that if someone did not believe in God, bring 'em to the Grand Canyon, and that will change their mind. And to seal the deal—watch a sunrise or sunset at the Grand Canyon.

I am simply amazed at the creation story, and I am not convinced or even impressed with any theory of creation, scientific or otherwise, that suggests that a divine and supreme being was not behind it all. But even more fascinating for me is that God has never stopped creating. God creates every second of our lives.

As wonderful and awesome as the above examples are, I believe that God's best creative work is in the small details of our lives: a sunny, cool day for a nice walk, a child saying "Daddy, I love you," a wife cooking a great meal,[3] someone opening the door for you, a co-worker's smile, or the urge to donate to a local charity in much need. As I said above, God never stops creating.

A part of God's creation work is that He also plans every second of every day of our lives. I liken this to a giant chess board. And there is a piece on the board for each one of us. He is constantly moving our pieces around, planning out our day and what will take place in our day.

God's creation is simply about His love for us and His intricate plan to bless us, shower His grace on us, and have an eternal relationship with each one of us.

We need to marvel each day at this creation we live in!

We need to be in awe each day of God's greatness!

We need to praise God each day for who He is and what He has done for each one of us.

We need to be ever grateful for how much God loves you and me.

Thought: How does God continue to create in your life?

Let us pray: Dear Heavenly God, we give You thanks and praise for Your creation work. Never allow us to take for granted what You have done and what You will do every day of our lives. You truly are an awesome God. Amen.

CREATION

---

[1] www.nursingassistance.com

[2] www.worldofhummingbirds.com

[3] And Gayle can cook some great meals: chicken pot pie and chili, just to name a couple

Day Two

FAITH

Now faith is confidence in what we hope for and assurance about what we do not see.

—Hebrews 11:1 NIV

FIRST, WE HOPE FOR MANY THINGS IN OUR LIVES. I HOPE THAT Clemson wins Saturday's football game.[1] Maybe you hope that this new dress will be appropriate for Easter service or you hope that you will pass your upcoming math test. However, the hope that the writer of the Book of Hebrews is referring to is the confident expectation that God will fulfill every promise he has made and that we are unconditionally sure and certain of this. Being confident is a good thing, right? We like confident people, not cocky or arrogant, but people who are sure about what they base their confidence on. The best example of this confidence is the true and sincere knowledge that there will come a day that we will spend eternity in heaven with loved ones and our creator.

Second, I have a friend who always replaces trust with faith. We have many things in our lives that we do not see, but we have trust in their existence. For example, we do not see gravity, but we know it exists because we remain planted firmly on the ground and do not go flying out in space. We do not see oxygen, but we know it is in the air because we breathe. And what about radio waves? Cell phones use radio waves to communicate. We cannot see those waves, but millions of people who have cell phones certainly know they exist. We have never seen God, never seen our Savior, Jesus, nor have we seen the Holy Spirit. But firm trust allows us Christians to accept the assurances in the Bible that the Trinity does exist.

God has made so many promises to us, such as the promises of His love for us, that He will never leave nor forsake us, and that He will give us hope and strength to endure our trials and tribulations. Real trust is being confident in our beliefs and placing our lives on these promises we have been given. You know, Jesus talked a lot about the faith of a child. And if you look at it, parents remember when their child or children were young. They knew for certain they were going to be taken care of. They did not just merely hope but were certain that Daddy would chase that monster out from under the bed or Mommy would fix that "boo-boo" after a fall. We parents provided the assurances and promises through what we said and did to give our children their trust in us. They did not have to go looking for it as they knew their parents' care would be there. How much more certain can we be in having the assurance in all that our great God has promised us.

This is how we need to approach our trust. Being confident in our salvation and being assured that heaven is real, that God created us, that Jesus died for us, and that the Holy Spirit is with us for guidance and direction. Having hope is the result of trusting God in everything, and having that hope simply gives us peace.

Thought: Think of a time when you could not see how a situation was going to work itself out, but you decided to trust in God anyway, and everything turned out alright.

Let us pray: Father God, You have promised us many things in scripture. Help us to always accept these promises without hesitation, without condition, and without reservation. You have given us hope, and this gives us the peace of mind that one day everything will be just fine. We trust You, Lord. Amen.

---

[1] My family and I are big Clemson Tiger fans. I "hope" you do not mind if I periodically use Clemson in this devotional book. No, just kidding, my Carolina Gamecock brothers and sisters.

Day Three

DO NOT COVET

Do not be overawed when others grow rich, when the splendor of their houses increases; for they will take nothing with them when they die, their splendor will not descend with them.

—Psalm 49:16–17 NIV

GOD HAS INSTRUCTED US IN THE TEN COMMANDMENTS THAT WE should not covet anything that our neighbors have. Have you taken that "hard look" at when our neighbors, our friends, build that big house, buy that fancy car, or put a Rolex on their wrist? I know that I have struggled with that from time to time and even covet what a member of my family may not have. I am certainly not condoning this, but I am just stating that it happens. On the reverse side, I am not saying that having "things" is bad. I believe that it is okay to be in "awe" and have an appreciation for what others have. But don't be "overawed," as the psalmist says, to the point of being consumed with some form of jealousy, a consuming yearning to possess what the neighbor or friend has. Quite honestly, I believe that this is what the Lord intended when He said, "Do not covet." Appreciate that new car, but don't let that appreciation develop into a desire to "have to have."

I believe the cure for those times that the appreciation level starts to develop into something more is Gratitude (with a capital G)—being appreciative for what we do have. All of us are blessed beyond measure, and we need to thank God for what He has given us.

Now, in the second part of this passage, the Psalmist makes a very simple but true statement that when we die, we take nothing with us. This rang so true for Gayle and me when my mother passed away. We went to my mother's house, and all of her things—her furniture, her clothes, all of her "do-dads" in the drawer next to her chair—were all there. Just as she left them. Nothing went in that casket with my mom from the house. She took nothing with her.

Eternal heaven is the treasure, and it means so much more than that house, car, or Rolex. So along with being careful of being in awe, we also need to think in terms of what is temporary and what is eternal. What has temporary value, and what has eternal value? Once we do this, then we can set our priorities where they need to be. What is most important first is our relationship with Jesus Christ. If that is our number one priority, then we can have some nice things after that.

When we are standing before Jesus, He is not going to ask us about how well those new golf clubs played or how many pairs of shoes we owned. No, He is going to ask us how grateful we have been for the many blessings in our lives and especially for the sacrifice that He made for us. That is what Jesus will be interested in.

Thought: Think of one thing you have that is temporary and one thing you have that is eternal.

DO NOT COVET

Let us pray: Dear Lord Jesus, keep our hearts filled with humble gratitude with a readiness to follow you always and to share Your love with others. Amen.

Day Four

THE WAY

Jesus answered, "I am the way and the truth and the life. No one comes to the Father except through me. If you really know me, you will know my Father as well. From now on, you do know him and have seen him."

—John 14:6–7 NIV

I AM OLD ENOUGH TO REMEMBER THE DAYS WHEN PAPER MAPS were used to get to an unknown destination. The map, when bought, was folded in the size of a long mailing envelope. When you unfolded it in the car, it would cover practically the entire dash and part of the front windshield.[1] Usually the wife had control over the map while riding shotgun in the passenger seat. Now, if the map was not getting you to your destination, there was a fallback plan usually advocated by the wife—stop at a convenience store or gas station for directions. If you husbands were like me, this plan was used only as a last resort. "Ask for directions? Never!" After driving aimlessly for hours, plan B would be put into effect.

Thank goodness we do not need maps anymore. We now have the luxury of GPS. What a life saver! And do you know what? I have yet to hear that lady in the GPS mechanism ever say, "We are lost! Can you pull into the next convenience store?" Praise God!

Jesus gives one of the strongest statements in scripture in answer to Thomas's question of where Jesus was going, as Thomas did not know the way. Jesus is telling Thomas and us that He is our GPS. He is the only way we get to heaven. He is the only Way we can see our heavenly Father, not just in heaven but now. Right now! Jesus wants us to know that He is our peace on earth. He gives us life to the fullest extent possible. What a wonderful thing that is to have Jesus guide us in every situation, to hold our hand in those fiery trials and predicaments we find ourselves in, and to clear those life paths that we allow to become overgrown! I know in my life Jesus has been my GPS so many times. In particular, several years ago, I was facing situations concerning a career path I was about to take. My nature has always been to take control myself, but after a while, I realized that I could not do it on my own because Jesus was telling me, "I have your back on this. Just follow my lead, and we will get through this together." You know what? We did!

You may ask, "How do I connect to Jesus as my GPS?" Very simply, spend time in prayer, meditation, and scripture reading. Open your heart up to Him and see what happens!

Thought: When was the last time you asked Jesus for help?

Let us pray: Lord Jesus, thank you for being my guide and protector. Help me always to seek You first and allow You to show me the way. Amen.

---

[1] Folding it back to its original size was an impossible feat. If any of you were able to, please call me so I can know how the magic trick was done.

Day Five

SIN

*Now I am about to go the way of all the earth. You know
with all your heart and soul that not one of all the good
promises the LORD your God gave you has failed. Every
promise has been fulfilled; not one has failed. But just as
all the good things the LORD your God has promised you
have come to you, so he will bring on you all the evil
things he has threatened, until the LORD your God has
destroyed you from this good land he has given you. If
you violate the covenant of the LORD your God, which he
commanded you, and go and serve other gods and bow
down to them, the LORD's anger will burn against you,
and you will quickly perish from the good land he has
given you.*

—Joshua 23:14–16 NIV
(Portion of Joshua's farewell
speech to the leaders of Israel)

JOSHUA WAS IN HIS LAST DAYS. HE GATHERED TOGETHER ALL OF
the leaders, elders, judges, and officials. Joshua was a man of
God, and he wanted his brethren to know first how great God

has been to them but on the flip side wanted to warn them what would happen if they continued in their sin.

When we read this passage, God, through Joshua, is speaking to us today. See, we have an extremely patient and loving God. Many believe that the reason for Jesus not returning yet is that God's patience is at its height, and he wants more and more people to accept Christ as Lord and Savior. But we have to be careful, very careful, that we do not interpret this patience as some sort of approval by God for our sinful ways or that He is somehow indifferent or even oblivious to our sins. Quite to the contrary, He is fully and totally aware of every sin we commit. Do not think we can hide, because we can't. Out of God's immense love for us, He calls on us to repent and return to Him each time we sin.

How do we know that God hates sin? We certainly have proof in that He allowed his Son, Jesus Christ, to die that horrible death on the cross. Jesus suffered, but also, I believe that God suffered as well since He was in the audience of those who watched Jesus die on the cross. See, forgiveness cannot take place without the Cross. Jesus had to take on our sins so our sins would die with Jesus. We still sin, though, but once we confess and repent of our sins, then forgiveness, through Jesus's death, is right there. Keep in mind, however, we must always be careful and not be complacent with our sins and God's reaction to our sins.

So there you have it. When we sin, there is a perfect recipe for God's forgiveness. We confess our sin, we repent of our sin, we seek His forgiveness, and we seek His help to change.

Thought: God still loves us unconditionally even when we sin.

Let us pray: Dear Loving God, thank you for being the loving and patient God that You are. You never ever fail us as Your promises are rock-solid, and we can rely on them every day of our lives. Help us when we sin with being fully remorseful with a desire to truly change. Amen.

Day Six

THE HEART

The LORD does not look at the things people look at. People look at the outward appearance, but the LORD looks at the heart.

—1 Samuel 16:7b NIV

HAVE YOU EVER HEARD THE SAYING "HE JUST DOES NOT HAVE HIS heart in it," or have you ever said, "I just do not have a heart for it anymore?" What we are saying here is that without the heart, there is no desire, no interest, no passion … just emptiness. But what about "that just warms my heart" or "bless his heart."[1] Or, as my son, Mike, was described at his Eagle Scout Court of Honor: "He has a big heart."

This passage deals with the Lord anointing David as King after "terminating" Saul. And just a few chapters preceding the above passage, David was referred to as a "Man after God's own heart." Scripture is full of references to the heart. So I would venture to say that the heart is a big deal to God.

I believe that the heart is the key to having a relationship with our Lord. He wants us to have a willing heart in finding and accepting His will in our lives. He does not simply want our time, energy, or even our money if our heart is not in it.

One of the worst situations that we all have unfortunately found ourselves in is during worship service. Our minds are all over the place, far removed from where our minds need to be—a focus on our worship of God. We have our minds on what we are going to have for lunch, the work agenda for the coming week, whether or not to pursue that investment strategy we read about that morning, all the while keeping an eye on the clock.

There are many different types of spiritual hearts that God wants us to have, and I believe that the two most important hearts to have are a grateful heart and a humble heart. We need to be passionately grateful to our Lord for all he has and will do for us, along with a willingness to give back to him to advance His kingdom here on this earth. We are sure that we never want God to say to us, "Is that all you are giving me, after all I have done for you? Really now?" The second heart is a humble heart. We humans are selfish. We humans are full of pride. We humans want to be in control and really believe that we are. Even though I am going to talk more about humility in another devotional, I believe a humble heart is a heart that recognizes our weaknesses and how much we are dependent on God. In all that we do, it must not be for our own glory but to honor and glorify God.

So how do we have and maintain these two hearts? I believe the first way to start is to serve others. Help in times of despair. Give in times of need. Pray in times of challenges. That, my friends, will be pleasing to God beyond measure.

Thought: We should always strive to have a heart connected to God.

Let us pray: Dear Father, help me to have that heart that wants to serve You, love You, and bring You all honor and glory. Help me too, Lord, to have that humble heart knowing that I cannot do life without You. Amen.

---

[1] Now read these two sayings again but with a little southern drawl. There you go, you've got it!

Day Seven

FRIENDSHIP

Greater love has no one than this: to lay down one's life for one's friends. You are my friends if you do what I command. I no longer call you servants, because a servant does not know his master's business. Instead, I have called you friends, for everything that I learned from my Father I have made known to you.

—John 15:13–15 NIV

GAYLE'S FATHER, ROBERT, WAS A PRISONER OF WAR DURING World War II in Germany, in what was known as Stalag IX-B. He was housed in deplorable and overcrowded conditions. The POWs were given very little food, and starvation was a result for many. Robert had a friend from the same area in South Carolina who was a prisoner in the same camp. Robert shared his food with this friend to help keep him alive. Robert risked his own life for his friend. Why? Robert's friend was married with children, and Robert was single without children. The friend survived and was able to enjoy his release along with Robert five months after capture. This friend credited Robert with saving his life.

This passage comes from Jesus talking to his disciples after the Last Supper. Wow, after they had spent three years with Jesus, who they considered their master, Jesus tells them that He now considers them his friends. That is pretty cool!

What is a true friend? I believe the list is quite endless. Allow me to give some examples.

A true friend will come to you at any time, day or night, when you are in a crisis.

A true friend will make you better simply because of the friendship.

A true friend will love you in spite of your faults.

A true friend will always give you a hug when you need it, and that hug is a mighty good one.

A true friend will serve all of your needs.

This passage from the Gospel of John reveals that Jesus is that true friend to all of us. He tells his disciples, and He is telling us that he wants to be that true friend because He loves us. I love the end of John's Gospel in the story of Jesus cooking breakfast on the shore of the Sea of Galilee. Think about this. Friendships were so important to Jesus that he wanted to spend His last days on this earth with His friends, His disciples. "Friends, haven't you any fish?" Jesus asks. (John 21:5 NIV)

Jesus also says to His disciples that He will be their friend if they do what He commands. Wait a minute! Conditional friendship? No! His command was to love one another. To serve one another. So, can we not then say that friendships and servanthood go hand in hand? Loving and serving each other is what friends do. That is what Christians do. That is what Jesus does. But we must remember that this is a two-way street. For any relationship to survive, for any friendship to be true and long-lasting, both sides must be willing to love and share. Each side must be willing to place the other's desires and wants over their own. Jesus has His end covered. Do we?

And Jesus says that I am going to "sweeten the pot" in our friendship. I am going to lay down my life for you, and for you, and for you!

Walt Whitman once said, "No doubt I have deserved my enemies, but no way I have deserved my friends."[1] We do not deserve Jesus's friendship, but it is certainly there for the taking! What a blessing!

Thought: Think of a true friend that you have that you have not talked with in a while. Give them a call.

Let us pray: Holy Lord Jesus, what a friend we have in you. Thank You for taking me as I am. Thank You for helping me, guiding me, and loving me. Thank You for being my friend. And Lord Jesus, help me be a good friend to others. Amen.

---

[1] www.azquotes.com

Day Eight

JUSTICE, MERCY, AND HUMILITY

He has shown you, O mortal, what is good. And what does the LORD require of you? To act justly and to love mercy and to walk humbly with your God.

—Micah 6:8 NIV

IF SOMEONE ASKED YOU TO ACT JUSTLY, SHOW SOME MERCY, AND act with humility, would you know what that means? This is one of those passages of scripture that is reasonably short but so powerful with so much meaning. Now, with many passages of scripture like this one, the Lord is telling the people of Israel how they should act. But while initially directed at the Hebrew people, I believe that it is being directed to us believers today. So let's unpack this little gem. Remember, it requires all three together or none at all.

First, when it says, "what does the Lord require," it is telling us we have no option. This is not a directive for us to act on a voluntary basis. This is not something that is being suggested for us to give it a try some time when the time is right. No, it is mandatory, and God expects us to conduct ourselves in these three ways. And if the truth were known, these are some pretty good things to do.

Act justly: We all want to be dealt with in a fair and honest manner. There is nothing worse than to be treated in the wrong way or having been taken advantage of. Injustice, real or perceived, can really have a harmful effect on us. Injustice simply is not a good thing. So if we want to be treated justly, we need to treat others in a just manner. As I am typing these words, I cannot help but think of Jesus when He was arrested and so horribly mocked and ridiculed by the Romans and even his own people, then brutally beaten and crucified. From one perspective, that is probably the greatest act of injustice known to mankind. Anyways, I believe that we are being told to be fair to others, be sensitive to their needs, help when help is needed, and do it out of love. This is how you act justly. One of my favorite quotes comes from the late Ravi Zacharias: "You can judge without loving, but you can't love without also being just."[1]

Love mercy: Mercy is simply forgiveness. What we all deserve many times over is done away with by God's forgiveness. The old saying "you get what you deserve" does not apply here.[2] God loves to forgive. It is a big deal with Him. That is why this passage tells us to love forgiveness! We need to embrace it! We need to feel it to our very core! And we need to practice it every day of our lives. How do we forgive a person who can be hard to forgive? Usually, it is not so much that the person is hard to forgive but that our resentment and anger are preventing us from forgiving the person. When we realize that "holding a grudge" is detrimental to our health, both physically and spiritually, we can begin to move toward forgiveness for that person. There is a Chinese proverb that says, "If you are going to pursue revenge, you better dig two graves." Let go, and I bet you will feel much better.

Walk humbly: If you could take one characteristic of a true, born-again Christian, I believe that characteristic would be humility. One of the best quotes defining humility is: "True humility is not thinking less of yourself, it is thinking of yourself less."[3] From a practical standpoint, there are many ways to show humility. Allow someone to go ahead of you in the grocery line when they have fewer items than you do. Admit your mistakes and recognize when you are wrong. Make a call to that elderly shut-in from church, knowing that this person has no family to make that call.

From a spiritual standpoint, we all need to recognize that we cannot "do life" without our heavenly creator to lean on. We need to simply replace our default reaction of being in control of the situation to allowing God to control. We need to have the mindset of a child, as Jesus tells us in the Gospel of Matthew.

So, what have we learned today? We need to simply treat others justly each day in the same way we want to be treated. Forgive others even when it is hard to do. Finally, have a humble attitude in all that we do.

Thought: Can you forgive that person today who has been so hard to forgive?

Let us pray: Please, Lord Jesus, give me that heart and mind that is full of love, of mercy, and of humility, willing to help my neighbor with a spirit of caring and fair-mindedness. Amen.

---

[1] *The Logic of God* (page 94)

[2] Man, if my parents knew half of the things I did growing up, it may not have been very pretty!

---

[3] Rick Warren, *The Purpose Driven Life: What on Earth Am I Here For?* Chapter 19.

Day Nine

JESUS WE HAVE NOT SEEN

Though you have not seen him, you love him; and even though you do not see him now, you believe in him and are filled with inexpressible and glorious joy, for you are receiving the end result of your faith, the salvation of your souls.

—1 Peter 1:8–9 NIV

I WOULD GUESS THAT JUST ABOUT ALL OF US LEARNED TO RIDE A bicycle just about the same way. We started off with training wheels, which helped us stay secure and upright on the bicycle. Then the big day came with the training wheels coming off.[1] You have your mom or dad behind you pushing you along. You cannot see them behind you, but you have faith that they are there, keeping you upright and ready to rescue you if the bicycle begins leaning dangerously to one side or the other.

This passage for today is like a pep talk, not only to those in the early church but to us even today. Peter is saying, "Guys, that is absolutely great! You have never seen Jesus as I have, but you love him as much as I do. And you know what, your faith is not only going to give you much joy, really wonderful joy right now, but it is going to save you!" I have to believe that Peter was just busting at the seams when he was writing these two verses with awe and wonder at their faith. And don't we have that same excitement and joy when we see someone come to faith in Christ? We do, and scripture tells us that even angels in heaven exhibit that same feeling.

Christianity is not about a system, a process, a way of doing things. No, it is about a person. It is about Jesus, who we have never seen, but our faith is still real. Simple as that. Just like mom and dad, who we could not see behind us, but we had faith they were there. It is the same with faith in Jesus, who we cannot see, but we know that He is there. And faith in Jesus allows us to love. It brings us joy and paves the way to heaven! I like simple things. Don't you?

Thought: When you learned to ride a bicycle, you had faith in your mom and dad, did you not? Do you have that same kind of faith in Jesus even though you have never seen Him?

Let us pray: Thank You, my Lord in heaven, that You gave me Your son, Jesus, who I know is with me every day, taking care of me, watching over me, and loving me as he does. Amen.

---

[1] With my kids, I was a little unorthodox. I took one training wheel off at a time. This would give them a little stability with one training wheel. And then at some point, the other one came off. My kids, especially Kathryn, still question my judgment to this day. I thought it was a good idea at the time.

Day Ten

ETERNITY

*He has made everything beautiful in its time. He has also
set eternity in the human heart; yet no one can fathom
what God has done from beginning to end.*

—Eccl. 3:11 NIV

HAVE YOU EVER MARVELED AT WHAT SOMEONE HAS ACCOMPLISHED
in their life, not understanding how the feat, record, invention,
or act was done? We are mystified, bewildered, and dumb-
founded. Back in October of 2012, an Austrian skydiver, Felix
Baumgartner,[1] performed a freefall from space (technically not
space—he was as high as 23 miles at the start, and space starts
at about 68 miles). Can you believe he was up that high when
he began to fall to Earth and, get this, traveling at speeds up to
729 mph?[2] I have watched the video, and while he did not
begin in space, it was mighty dark where he began. Near the
end of the fall, of course, a giant parachute emerged, and he
safely landed on the ground. But probably the most amazing
thing about this stunt was that he landed presumably where he
wanted to because several crew members and a helicopter were
right there to greet daring Felix. I don't know about you, but if I
get a couple of stories up in a building and look out the win-

dow, I get a little nervous. While I do not understand how this skydiver pulled this stunt off, I can still truly say that is one heck of an accomplishment by this courageous man!

This passage of scripture in the NIV uses the word "fathom." Fathom means something is difficult to understand after much thought. It is hard to understand sometimes what God has done throughout the ages. We are unable to completely understand the magnitude of His work from the beginning of creation to the present time and to the end of time. Why? Well, I think we know the answer. God is simply way smarter than we are, so His plan is to give us just enough to keep us going and not a bit more. He knows what we can handle and what is best for us.

But the great thing this passage also tells us is that there is a heaven, a place where all believers will spend eternity with our Father. How do we know that? We know it because it is on our hearts, delicately put there but also purposely placed there by God. How has He done it? How did He create this infinite place we will call home after we end this life on Earth? Don't know! Would we like to know? Well, maybe so. Maybe at least give us a little bit more about what heaven will be like—a little more than what Jesus tells us in scripture. But at the end of the day, we know that it will be a great place where Jesus will be. He promised us that. And we should never think of eternity in a quantitative way—how much time eternity is. We should always think of eternity in a qualitative way—how good it will be in heaven.

Dr. David Jeremiah said, "There will be a last night for every person, a last night for every nation. There will be a last meal, a last statement, a last breath and then … eternity."[3] Eternity is there for everyone, and hopefully for you, it is heaven.

But let's not worry too much if we do not understand all there is to know about God. Do you think we could handle it if we knew everything? We just need to accept the great God that we have, accept His awesome power and love, and be amazed of what God has in store for us. So, when the time comes, we will most definitely have a very safe landing in His loving arms! A safe landing just like good ole' Felix had.

Thought: When you hear the word "eternity," what is the first thing that comes to mind? Is it "man, that is a long time!" or is it "man, that will be a great time!"?

Let us pray: Dear Lord, You are a great God that creates, sustains, and loves all at the same time. Keep me keenly aware and never allow me to forget how awesome You are and that You have waiting for me a heavenly banquet, an eternal paradise that is simply going to be amazing. Amen.

---

[1] Wikipedia

[2] I bet that his spacesuit was rather warm on the outside!

[3] Online devotional, *Turning Point*, October 2, 2019

Day Eleven

A MERCIFUL, LOVING GOD

But because of his great love for us, God, who is rich in mercy, made us alive with Christ even when we were dead in transgressions—it is by grace you have been saved.

—Ephesians 2:4–6 NIV

HAVE YOU EVER HEARD THE STATEMENT, "WELL, THAT JUST SAYS it all"? This statement refers to something that very clearly shows the truth about a situation. Can you hear a football coach say, "We were not at our best here, and that says it all about how we are playing"? Or when a child says, "When I asked Dad if he was mad at me, his silence said it all"? How about the mom finding the cookies gone in the cookie jar, and she says, "That look of guilt on Timmy's face just said it all"?

This statement from Paul in Ephesians is one of those passages in scripture that "just says it all." Paul talks not just about God's love but His great love for us. It is God's great love that fuels everything that He has done for us and will do for us. According to the Gospel of John, it was out of this love that He sent Jesus to us. It was out of this great love that He would allow Jesus to die that horrific death on the cross for us. It is out of this great love that He extends his merciful hand to us, showing compassion, fully knowing that we do not deserve His mercy but deserve to be punished for our sinful and selfish ways. It is out of this great love that we have been forgiven for our sins, and through the Holy Spirit's sanctifying cleansing, we have been set apart and renewed with the blood of Jesus Christ. It is out of this great love that God has showered His grace on us, not because we have earned it or deserve it, but because this is who God is. The salvation of my soul and yours fully reveals this great love of God.

This bundle of love, mercy, and grace—what more could we ask for? It is because of this bundle that our sins have been forgiven, and we will spend eternity in the loving arms of our creator. That gives us peace. That gives us hope. Can't ask for anything more. That just says it all!

Thought: When was the last time you really felt God's love?

Let us pray: Dear Lord, I am not deserving of Your love, but You love me anyway. You extend me mercy when I have acted so contrary to Your plan for me. You pour Your grace out on me time after time, even though I continue to sin. Lord, give me a heart that will cause me to run after You and soak in what You have to offer me as Your child. Amen.

Day Twelve

PAUL'S SORROW AND ANGUISH

*I speak the truth in Christ—I am not lying, my con-
science confirms it through the Holy Spirit—I have great
sorrow and unceasing anguish in my heart. For I could
wish that I myself were cursed and cut off from Christ for
the sake of my people, those of my own race.*

—Romans 9:1–3 NIV

THIS IS ONE OF THOSE PASSAGES THAT EVERY TIME I READ IT, I AM
blown away! I am, quite frankly, overwhelmed with amazement that someone would even state that they would offer
themselves eternal hell for a person or persons coming to
Christ. Who would do that? So when I read this passage from
Paul's letter to the Romans, I ask myself if I would be willing to
do the same thing? Would I substitute myself for eternal dam-
nation in return for someone receiving eternal heavenly bliss?
Would I even make such a statement? Sadly and honestly, I
would have to say no. What would you say? This shows how
strong Paul's compassion was for his fellow man. It shows how

concerned—truly concerned—he was for his brothers and sisters and where their faith was.

I believe that if we carefully look at this passage, it goes beyond what always "blows me away." First, it reminds us that there is only one way to salvation, and that is through our Lord and Savior, Jesus Christ. A hundred people willingly going to hell to save one person is not what it takes to get that one person into heaven. For the apostle Paul, a great man of faith, going to hell would not put his people in heaven. Paul knew this, but it still does not diminish the sorrow and disappointment that he felt in his heart for his people.

Secondly, it should cause us to look inward to find out where our hearts are when it comes to people we know who are not saved. What do we do about it? We should have that same sorrowful heart as Paul. We should have that same concern and should therefore have that same desire to help. We often think we are not successful in helping people come to Christ if they do not experience right then a "Damascus-road experience" or something akin to that. If we just plant that "seed," that idea, in their minds, then God can take it from there. Give a Bible, make an invitation to church, set an example, tell someone how important your faith is to your life and well-being—that is all it takes. First, have the heart and concern, and then just take that next step, however small that step may be.

Thought: Do you know someone that needs a seed planted?

Let us pray: Lord, there is a lot of work to do in Your kingdom. Give me the heart to help those who do not know You. Give me the concern for the future well-being of those who do not live the gospel. Guide and direct me to do something. Amen.

Day Thirteen

EYES ON JESUS

Fixing our eyes on Jesus, the pioneer and perfecter of faith. For the joy set before him he endured the cross, scorning its shame, and sat down at the right hand of the throne of God.

—Hebrews 12:2 NIV

DID YOU KNOW THAT OUT OF ALL OF THE MEMBERS OF THE ANIMAL kingdom, the eagle has the best eyesight—up to eight times better than humans? They can spot a rabbit two miles away. That is where we get the term "eagle eye."[1]

As the eagle stays focused on that rabbit, we need to stay focused on Jesus. When the author of Hebrews says, "fixing our eyes on Jesus," he does not mean just looking at or for Jesus. No, he means placing all of our faith and love in Jesus. One of my favorite authors, Tim Keller, said it best in one of his books,[2] where he writes: "Please don't try to keep Jesus on the periphery of your life. He can't remain there. Give yourself to Him— center your entire life on Him—and let His power reproduce His character in you."

Sadly we are all blind at times. Often, it is self-imposed. We do not see Jesus for who He is and allow Him to show us the way. Often, however, it is the cares of the world and the clutter that our culture fills our minds with that causes this spiritual blindness. Now, if you really think about it, why were there so many stories in the Bible about blind people? Jesus healed them, and we need to allow Jesus to heal us too. Heal us so we can keep that focus. Heal us so that when we wander and stray off of the path, we will allow Jesus to reel us back in. Heal us so that we can experience that joy—not just the joy that Jesus can bring us now, but the joy that Jesus experiences being right next to his Father. The joy that got Jesus through that terrible ordeal on the cross. The joy that will get us through any trouble, problem, or tragedy that comes our way.

I think we all need to say every day, "I see you Jesus. I am coming your way! Please take my hand and help me there!"

Thought: Do you ever feel like the cares of this world cause you to have blinders on and that you really do not see?

Let us pray: Dear Lord Jesus, we pray for eagle eyes so that we can see You clearly, and then You show us the way. When we wander, when we stray, and when we are blind to your love, set us straight and help us to see. Amen.

---

[1] I always thought my Dad had the eyesight of an eagle. Growing up, he could spot things I was doing, and I was not anywhere close to the house. That always amazed me.

[2] *King's Cross* at page 162

LIFE'S RACE

I have fought the good fight, I have finished the race, I have kept the faith. Now there is in store for me the crown of righteousness, which the Lord, the righteous judge, will award to me on that day—and not only to me, but also to all who have longed for his appearing.

—2 Timothy 4:7–8 NIV

MY DAUGHTER, KATHRYN, WAS QUITE THE ATHLETE IN HIGH school. One of her sports was track, and she excelled in the 4 X 100 relay. This is the sprint relay in which each of the four runners runs 100 meters and then hands off the baton to the next runner. Kat ran the third leg of the relay, which consisted of running around the last of the two curves on the track, and man, when she grabbed that baton from runner number two, it was a thing of beauty. She was not a tall girl at all, but she had mastered the stride, and she could fly. She only had 100 meters to run, and she pushed herself, giving it everything she had. Then she had someone to take the baton from her. What a race to see, and her relay team was pretty good!

The spiritual race that we run and the spiritual race that Paul ran are different from Kathryn's relay race. Ours is not a sprint but a marathon: a long journey with many hills and valleys. Life is difficult in so many ways, and we have all experienced those trials and tribulations. Sickness, tragedy, and death have all pierced our lives in some fashion. They did for the apostle Paul. However, his beatings, imprisonments, and perils at sea did not stop Paul from spreading the gospel message.

I am reminded of the Rocky movies, in which Rocky gets knocked down multiple times and, each time he gets up, motions to Apollo Creed with his boxing glove as if to say, "Come on, bring it on!" We have a God who is a great God! And we need to rely on the power of His Holy Spirit to get through life's challenges so we can say, "Come on, bring it on!"

Paul recognizes, as all believers do, that there is a light at the end of that tunnel. There is a pot of gold at the end of that rainbow. That pot, that light, is Paul's crown, and our crown of righteousness when we will be with our heavenly creator. That is the trophy that we will get one day. During our faith journey, we need to constantly fight against the evils of our world and continue to persevere and keep our faith strong.

When life gets tough, when we stumble, and when we face adversity, we simply need to get up, brush ourselves off, and continue toward that finish line. When we reach that finish line, we are going to be tired and out of breath. But you know who will be at that finish line—our Lord and Savior, Jesus Christ, who will grab hold of us and say, (and I cannot wait to hear these words) "You have fought hard and have kept the faith, and now you have finished. Come across my good and faithful servant."

Can I get an amen to that?

Thought: Are you running in a race right now? If you are, what kind of race is it? Are you pushing hard and keeping the faith? Are you relying on the power of Jesus?

Let us pray: Lord, You are a gracious and loving God who understands my shortcomings, my failures, and my weakness in faith at times. But when I fall, please help me up and remind me to faithfully keep going, knowing one day that You will be there at the end of my life's race. Amen.

Day Fifteen

RICHES AND POVERTY

Two things I ask you, LORD; do not refuse me before I die: Keep falsehood and lies far from me; give me neither poverty nor riches, but give me only my daily bread. Otherwise, I may have too much and disown you and say, 'Who is the LORD?' Or I may become poor and steal, and so dishonor the name of my God.

—Proverbs 30:7–9 NIV

MY WIFE, GAYLE, OF 45 YEARS OF MARRIAGE, HAS ALWAYS HAD the desire to provide for her family. She has done this for me, our children, our grandchild, and her parents. She is a great cook, and there was always a great meal on the table when my kids were growing up. She made sure that they were fed. And to this day, she still cooks meals and provides food for my grown children. I know that she is horrified when she thinks one of her kids is hungry. To this day, she feeds me pretty well, too. Additionally, Gayle checks in on and takes care of her 93-year-old mother, who lives in a local nursing home. She has taken care of her and her father when he was alive through their time in hospitals, rehabilitation, and when they were together in the same nursing home. She simply has that knack, along with the desire, to provide what is needed. As much as she loves her parents, I think her favorite person to dote on is our grandson.

Boy, is this not just like our Father in heaven? The author of today's passage nailed it. "Lord, do not give me too much or too little." Why make that request? Because God knows exactly what we need, and we need to have that recognition that God knows exactly what we need. But it is hard sometimes, isn't it? The culture that we live in encourages, promotes, and emphasizes that "more is better." You are successful if you have a lot. You are going to be happier with more. That big house, fancy car, money in the bank—that is a sure sign of a winner.

Now, let's go back to today's passage. If we put anything above God, then we have a problem, right? Right. It is not that God does not want us to have things. He sure does want us to have things. We just must make sure that we have our priorities right and place God before everything else. Make sure He is at the center of our lives. Otherwise, it is an act of "disowning," which is a fairly strong term. Look at the definition: "a refusal to acknowledge or maintain any connection with." Even though we do at times disown, I do not believe there is a believer out there who would say that is something we mean to do. But, once again, we do it, don't we? Now, on the other side of the coin, if we have too little, then we may do something, like stealing, that is not only a sin but also brings dishonor to our Lord. We simply dishonor Him when we sin. And when we sin, we need to recognize that sin, then seek forgiveness with a remorseful heart and seek the Holy Spirit's guidance to change.

So what is the bottom line of all of this? We need to know that God, who is Number One, will provide exactly what we need, not what we want or think we need. Often, it is so very hard to be satisfied, but satisfaction is the spot where God wants us to be. Just as Gayle loves to provide, so does our heavenly Father love to provide for His children.

Thought: Do you think you have too little, and if so, why? Where do you think this dissatisfaction is coming from?

Let us pray: Dear Father in Heaven, You are the provider and sustainer of all life and everything that is a part of life. Please, every day, help me to be humbly grateful for what You have given me, how You have blessed me, and how You have filled my cup overflowing with Your love and grace. Amen.

WORDS FROM THE HEART

*If you declare with your mouth, "Jesus is Lord," and be-
lieve in your heart that God raised him from the dead,
you will be saved. For it is with your heart that you believe and are justified, and it is with your mouth that you
profess your faith and are saved.*

—Romans 10:9–10 NIV

THERE IS A STORY ABOUT A ZOO THAT WAS FAMOUS FOR HAVING A
great variety of different animals. One day, the gorilla died. To
keep up the appearance of a full range of animals, the zookeep-
er hired a man to wear a gorilla suit to fill in for the dead animal. It was the first day on the job, and the man did not really
know how to act like a gorilla. As he tried to move around like
a gorilla, he got too close to the wall of the enclosure, tripped,
and fell into the lion exhibit. He started screaming, knowing
that he was going to die, until the lion spoke to him: "Be quiet,
or you are going to get us both fired."

Every time I read today's passage from Paul's letter to the Romans, I am reminded of the Gospel of Matthew in Chapter 7, where Jesus says, "Not everyone who says to me, Lord, Lord, will enter the kingdom of heaven." Jesus was certainly exposing the "religious" leaders of the day, who definitely put on appearances and talked a great game. Would it be fair to say that the "religious" leaders of Jesus's day were a lot like the men in the animal costumes? We learn that we need to be careful and mean what we say, not just for how it looks. Otherwise, the consequences can be dreadful.

I believe there are two points that Paul is really focused on in today's passage. First, we must be willing to profess and share our faith. Second, we need to make sure that we have a sincere heart to back up our profession of faith.

We must not be shy about sharing our faith with others. So many times, we are so tight-lipped with our faith for fear of ridicule or even persecution that we do not say anything, especially in a time that begs for something to be said. We must never hesitate to tell people that Jesus is Lord, as He died on the cross for the forgiveness of our sins and, along with sincerely expressing with our words, we must back our words up with action. We are on this earth to serve in order to bring honor and glory to our God.

Additionally, we do not want our words to be empty. We want our words backed up with a true and sincere heart. In a prior devotion, I talked about how important our heart is to our faith journey. Without the heart, our words simply cannot have any meaning. I love the story of the Pharisee and the tax collector at the temple praying as found in Chapter 18 in the Gospel of Luke. It was the Pharisee who was like the zoo and the men in the gorilla and lion suits—simply creating appearances. It was the tax collector who had his heart into the prayer.

So let's be bold and be willing to witness and profess our faith. Do it with a humble heart for Jesus, knowing for certain that He died for us and also came alive for us so that we can have the opportunity to live eternally with Him. Oh, what a blessing!

Thought: Has there been a time when you realized that you were simply concerned with appearances regarding your faith? Was it maybe due to your heart not being in it at the time?

Let us pray: Dear Lord Jesus, give me the strength and courage to be a disciple of Yours willing to declare that You loved us so much that You went to the cross for us. And give me the heart to love You back and be so ever grateful that our Father in heaven raised You from the tomb and gave You life so that we could have life eternal. Amen.

Day Seventeen

THE CROSS

Surely he took up our pain and bore our suffering, yet we considered him punished by God, stricken by him, and afflicted. But he was pierced for our transgressions, he was crushed for our iniquities; the punishment that brought us peace was on him, and by his wounds we are healed. We all, like sheep, have gone astray, each of us has turned to our own way; and the LORD has laid on him the iniquity of us all.

—Isaiah 53:4–6 NIV

THE CROSS IS THE CENTERPIECE OF THE CHRISTIAN FAITH—THE focal point of a believers' forgiveness of sins. Without the cross, we, my friends, have nothing.

When I think about Jesus on the day of His death, I often have mixed feelings. On the one hand, I am so deeply saddened that He was beaten, ridiculed, and tortured, then left nailed to the cross to die. I realize with shame that He had this done to Him because of me and because of you. God went to this extreme and witnessed His son's terrible death for sinful, selfish me. It is almost as if I think that I am one of those brutal Roman soldiers who crucified Jesus.

On the other hand, I feel a strong sense of gratitude. A couple of years ago, I started in my daily prayers thanking Jesus for dying for me and then thanking Him for coming alive for me. This strong sense of thankfulness usually overshadows any sadness or shame I feel.

When I experience this appreciation, I tend to add to it some amazement. This is what I mean: Here Jesus is, hanging on the cross with nails in His hands and feet, beaten to a pulp. His bloody human body, wrought with gashes, exposing bone and tissue, and yet Jesus, our sweet Jesus, still shows that He still has compassion and love until His last breath. He still asks God to forgive those people who were killing Him. He brings peace to the criminal by saving him. He asks John to take care of His mother. On the worst day of Jesus' life as a human being separated from God and hit with every sin of humankind, He still shows His love and His saving grace to others.

So I believe there is a lesson here. Paul tells us in Romans 8:28 that "in all things God works for [our] good." So, when troubles are all around us, our day gets gloomier by the minute, and we shout, "Woe is me!" We need to pause and remember Jesus on the cross. We need to be grateful for what Jesus did for us and be eternally thankful to Him. God can take what appears to be a bad situation and turn it into good. He took that horrible day of the cross and turned it into a fantastic day for mankind. God can do this for us. Above, Paul says, "in ALL things (emphasis added)." God can turn whatever negative there is in our lives and make it a positive. We should never hesitate to say, "Thank You!"

Thank You, God!

Thought: No matter how bad your day is, being truly thankful can make things better.

Let us pray: Lord Jesus, I do thank You for dying for me, and I do thank You for coming alive for me. Never let a day go by for me that I do not thank You for what You have done for me. Keep my heart full of gratitude and humility. Amen.

Day Eighteen

WHO AM I?

Once when Jesus was praying in private and his disciples were with him, he asked them, "Who do the crowds say I am?" They replied, "Some say John the Baptist; others say Elijah; and still others, that one of the prophets of long ago has come back to life." "But what about you?" he asked. "Who do you say I am?" Peter answered, "God's Messiah."

—Luke 9:18–20 NIV

I HEARD A STORY ONCE ABOUT A FAMOUS DOCTOR IN ENGLAND. HE was riding on a passenger train, and the train conductor was punching tickets. When the conductor got to the doctor, the doctor reached into his vest pocket but had no ticket. He reached into his pants pocket, but no ticket. He looked in his briefcase, but still no ticket. Lastly, he looked in the seat next to him: no ticket.

The train conductor said, "Dr. Johnson, I know who you are. Everyone knows who you are. I am sure that you purchased a ticket, so no problem." The doctor nodded in appreciation, and the train conductor proceeded to punch the remaining tickets. When he had finished, he turned around, and he saw the doctor on his hands and knees looking for the ticket. He rushed back to the doctor's seat and said, "Dr. Johnson, again, I know who you are, and it still is no problem that you cannot find your ticket.

The doctor responded, "Young man, I too know who I am. What I do not know is where I am going."

I believe there are two lessons here to grasp hold of. The first lesson is how much concern we have for what others think of us. How much we strive for that acceptance—that recognition from others. When I preach a sermon, I really struggle with being more concerned with what others think of my sermon than what God thinks of my sermon. I have to constantly ask God to help me put my focus in the proper direction—on Him. So if we were to ask others, "Hey, what does John think of me?" or "Mary, who does she say I am?" that would be a form of pride, would it not? On the one hand, having a good reputation in the community and wanting to have that good reputation is not a bad thing. Being obsessed with it is probably a bad thing, and more importantly, putting this above what God thinks of us and who God says we are is the sin that we must all avoid. I have said in a previous devotion the best thing ever is Jesus calling me and calling you, "My good and faithful servant." That is where we need to put our attention.

The second lesson is that Jesus asks us every day, "Do we know where we are going?" He is seeking that confession from us. The answer to that question really depends on how we answer the next question from Jesus: "Who do you say I am?"

Do we say, "You are my Lord, my Savior, and also my friend?" He knows what is on our hearts, but He wants us to have that inner reflection—that inner soul-searching of where our faith is. Our response has eternal consequences as it did with Peter and the disciples. Our recognition of Jesus being our Savior who died that horrible death on the cross so our sins would be forgiven is the most important recognition that our minds will ever make. It is the most important acknowledgment that our hearts will ever truly feel and believe. So if we know where we are going when life ends on this earth for us, then the answer is crystal clear to the question of truly knowing who Jesus is.

Thought: When Jesus asks you, "Who do you say I am?" do you respond with, as Peter did, "My Messiah?"

Let us pray: Dear Jesus, help me to always accept You as my messiah and Savior, knowing where I am going for my eternal destination when my life ends on this earth. Amen.

Day Nineteen

WHAT GOD PROVIDES

May the God of hope fill you with all joy and peace as you trust in him, so that you may overflow with hope by the power of the Holy Spirit.

—Romans 15:13 NIV

FIVE KEY WORDS/PHRASES JUMP OUT AT ME WHEN I READ TODAY'S passage: hope, joy, peace, trust, and power of the Holy Spirit. I will address each one and take them slightly out of order.

Trust: Trust is the starting point for every Christian's spiritual journey. Without trusting God's promises, without trusting the sovereignty of God, and without trusting the love that God showers on his children, I do not believe that hope, joy, and peace are even possible. In addition to trust, the power of His Holy Spirit is essential to fill us with these wonderful gifts.

Hope: There are many great things about being a Christian, but the one that stands out time after time is the hope we have for eternal life in heaven with our Lord and Savior, Jesus Christ. This hope is solid and real. Christ died on the cross for the forgiveness of sins and came alive three days later so that we could also experience a resurrected life in heaven. It is so exciting for believers to have this hope of life after death. Death is not the victor here. The hope that we have and rely on throughout our lives is God's promise that we will one day be in His glory.

Joy: Many people say that this "biblical" joy is not just being happy about things but being content, being satisfied, and feeling very good about your relationship with the Lord and your relationships with others. I totally agree. I liken this joy to the feeling that you had when you first saw that newly born child or grandchild. Sure, you were happy, but that happiness went to the next level. The joy that only the Lord can give is that joy that makes you complete and ready to share with others. It's that joy causing a feeling so "you lack for nothing" and know whatever the world has to offer will never compare to the joy we have in the Lord.

Peace: People often say, " I am at peace with it." It is usually said when a loved one dies. There is something to be said about this phrase. It means they are comfortable with and accepting of the outcome that has transpired or the ultimate outcome not yet taken place. There is no question God's hand is all over the person, and they have placed it with God. I remember when I had my cancer surgery, and a person commented on how Gayle and I were completely at peace waiting in the hospital room for the nurse to wheel me back to the operating room. We just gave it to God and allowed Him to take control. It was that trust in God and who God is. We knew that God was with us and would never leave us. We also knew that God was with the surgeon and medical team in the surgery room so that I would receive the best care possible. We never doubted. Without doubt, there can always be this peace, this everlasting and assuring peace.

Holy Spirit: None of this could be possible without the indwelling power of the Holy Spirit within our hearts. We have the Holy Spirit when we are saved, and when we allow the Holy Spirit to work in our lives, then the more peace, more joy, and more hope we will experience. This is God's glory at work! Hallelujah!

Thought: How much joy, peace, and hope do you want to have today? Allow the Holy Spirit to work in your life!

Let us pray: Dear God, it is because You love us so much that You want us to experience Your joy, peace, and hope. For that, we are so thankful. As we continue our faith journey with You, help us to submit daily to the awesome power of Your Holy Spirit. May we always bring You honor and glory. Amen.

Day Twenty

DO NOT FEAR

*So do not fear, for I am with you; do not be dismayed, for
I am your God. I will strengthen you and help you; I will
uphold you with my righteous right hand.*

—Isaiah 41:10 NIV

IN DECEMBER OF 2019, I HAD A FALL AND WAS TAKEN TO THE LOCAL
hospital. Because my injuries required a specialist, I was taken
to another hospital about 35 miles away. This was late at night.
Since I had to be transported by ambulance,[1] my wife, Gayle,
had to drive herself. It was late at night and rainy. To top it all
off, Gayle also had her mother in the local hospital. Needless to
say, her fear and anxiety levels were at their peak. But what got
her through the ordeal to the hospital, she tells me, was this
passage from Isaiah. She tells me she repeated this passage over
and over as she was driving in those not-so-welcoming conditions. Because she did this, she got through the drive, and her
fear and anxiety levels continued to subside.

In this passage, God commands the Israelites not to fear,
but He is also telling us in this passage not to fear as well. He
assures us that he will give us the strength and help we need to
get through whatever situation that we are in. Why should we

put our faith into this promise? Because He is God. The creator and sustainer of all life has made this promise, so we should never hesitate to take this promise of strength and help as absolute fact. Do you remember what we discussed in the Day One devotion? God created Mount Everest, the human brain, the tiny hummingbird, and the Grand Canyon. If He can do all that, then we should be fairly comfortable in believing that He can lessen the fear and anxiety that an upset and worried wife of mine had while driving in poor nighttime conditions.

God's right hand is mentioned multiple times in scripture and in Isaiah. Isaiah calls it in this passage a "righteous" right hand. Righteous means morally correct and justifiable. God certainly is the epitome and perfect example of being good and virtuous. Then, in Verse 13, God says that He will take "hold of your right hand." So picture this with me. You are in crisis — a bad situation. You simply look up to the Lord, and He knows what you need. Then that big, good, and loving right hand of His comes down and grabs hold of your right hand and brings you to safety so close to Him. That is the God we have. Full of love and righteousness. Full of care and concern for His children. That is the God we have, and for that we should "fear not!"

Thought: Think of a time when you experienced that grip of fear, you sought the Lord, and the fear went away. Being able to breathe a lot easier was a really good feeling, was it not?

Let us pray: Help us Lord to always seek You when we are in a crisis — when we are fearful not knowing what lies ahead. You are a great God. Thank You for taking care of us and loving us as much as you do. Amen.

---

[1] Boy, did I advocate for personal car transportation, but the doctors won out!

Day Twenty-One

GOD'S GOODNESS

The LORD bless you and keep you; the LORD make his face shine on you and be gracious to you; the LORD turn his face toward you and give you peace.

—Numbers 6:24–26 NIV

Now may the God of peace, who through the blood of the eternal covenant brought back from the dead our Lord Jesus, that great Shepherd of the sheep, equip you with everything good for doing his will, and may he work in us what is pleasing to him, through Jesus Christ, to whom be glory for ever and ever. Amen.

—Hebrews 13:20–21 NIV

May the grace of the Lord Jesus Christ, and the love of God, and the fellowship of the Holy Spirit be with you all.

—2 Corinthians 13:14 NIV

I LOVE A GOOD BENEDICTION. I COULD NOT DECIDE BETWEEN THESE three, so you get all three! We typically hear them in church, at the conclusion of the service, and if done correctly, it will sum up what has been the focus of the service (and sermon). The above three benedictions are some of the best found in scripture, and they have some similar themes, but I want to focus on just one: "the goodness of God," found in all three of these benedictions.

I am sure you are familiar with this. One person says, "God is good!" Then the other person (or persons) says, "All the time!" While some may think that this is a little corny, not for what is being said but how it is being said, I am here to tell you that this simple statement is exactly what these benedictions are telling us.

Our good God gave His children His child, Jesus, the great shepherd who went to the cross for his sheep, and the great shepherd who intercedes for His sheep in heaven every single day. Jesus, who provides us with the way, the only way, to our Father.

Our good God blesses His children. How? God showers us with His favor—His acts of kindness and generosity, those things in our lives that we do not deserve. For example, some may have great families, great friends, or great health. What did we do to earn these things in our lives? We did nothing (other than maybe eating right or exercising from time to time on the health issue). We may think that we can justify receiving the credit, but we cannot. Those good things in our lives that simply make us smile are all from God.

Our good God gives His children peace: a calm assurance of mind and spirit trusting in the awesome power of God, approaching everything in life in oneness with God and His Holy Spirit.

Our good God gives His children grace. It is because God loves us so much that He gives grace through peace and blessing to us. It is because of this unconditional love that He has always had for us that He gave up his son to die for us. This grace we cannot earn, nor do we deserve it. It is absolutely due to this grace that we receive God's peace, kindness, generosity, and His son, Jesus.

The goodness of God! Yes, God is good all of the time! For sure!

Thought: Do you ever ponder the goodness of God? How great and amazing it is!

Let us pray: Oh, our good, good God, how loving You are. How full of grace You are. Your mercy endures forever. Your peace comforts us. Your kindness and generosity are in abundant supply. Never let us take for granted all of what You have and will do for us. Please, Lord, give us thankful and obedient hearts. Amen.

Day Twenty-Two

COMMITMENT
TO GOD

*And now, Israel, what does the LORD your God ask of
you but to fear the LORD your God, to walk in obedience
to him, to love him, to serve the LORD your God with all
your heart and with all your soul, and to observe the
LORD's commands and decrees that I am giving you today for your own good?*

—Deuteronomy 10:12–13 NIV

THIS INSTRUCTION TO FEAR, OBEY, LOVE, AND SERVE GOD CAME
from Moses right after he came down from the mountain with
the second set of stone tablets containing the Ten Commandments. God told Moses to lead his people to the promised land.
This instruction also appears several times in other passages in
Deuteronomy. This passage reminds us of Jesus's declaration
that the greatest commandment is to love God with your heart,
soul, and mind. So what is Moses telling us? What is Jesus telling us? What is expected of us? Let's find out.

This passage is like an instruction book telling us how we ought to live our lives. Instruction books are good when trying to put something together, especially when one is not very handy.[1] Instruction books are good for our spiritual lives, especially since we tend to lead sinful lives at times.

Obey, fear, love, and serve! This instruction creates a challenge for us. Before we accept this challenge, we must first have the mindset that God is an absolutely awesome God, a completely sovereign God, a God full of greatness, and also a very generous God. We must believe this in our hearts. When we do this, then we will realize that everything God does is for our good. We will want to obey Him and follow every one of His commands. We will want to love Him with all of our hearts, and we will want to serve Him with reverence and respect.

Our instruction manual tells us to be committed. With any relationship, there must be total commitment both ways. Whether in marriage between spouses, in jobs between employer and employee, or in the sports world between coach and player. For the relationship to be productive, positive, and thriving, there must be commitment. In our relationship with our heavenly Father, there must be commitment.

There is no question that God is committed to us. We know that He loves us immensely, blesses us abundantly, and serves us daily by washing our feet with His grace and mercy. We, in return, must simply give our hearts to God. When Jesus said, "Follow me," he did not suggest that we come along half-heartedly without enthusiasm and spirit. No, he wants us to come to him giving our 110% being fully devoted and dedicated, coming to Him and living with Him, ready to obey, to love, and to serve!

Thought: Is commitment to God in your toolbox?

Let us pray: Holy Spirit, we need You today and every day to fill our souls with your guidance and direction to obey God, to love God, and to serve God. Help us to take up the cross and follow our Savior, Jesus. Amen.

---

[1] I am not handy at all! I have a detached garage at my house that I call The Shop. It makes you think that I have woodworking tools to make furniture and mechanic's tools to repair small engines in it. Nope!

WASHING AWAY OUR SINS

*He saved us, not because of righteous things we had
done, but because of his mercy. He saved us through the
washing of rebirth and renewal by the Holy Spirit.*

—Titus 3:5 NIV

WHY IS IT THAT WE GO THROUGH CYCLES IN LIKING TO TAKE
baths? When very young, a bath is so enjoyable. I know it is for
my grandson, Ford, who at the time of this writing is twenty-
three months old. He will splash and play and have so much
fun. Then as one gets a little older, it is a fight to get that child
to take a bath, especially the dirtier they are from playing outside. Then as an adult, baths (or better yet, showers) are so re-
freshing and soothing. I can stand there for, as it seems, hours
on end and let the water ease that tired back of mine.

In today's passage, Paul tells us that at the moment of our
acceptance of Christ as our Savior, we receive a divine shower,
if you will. A complete cleansing of all of our sins, done
through the renewing power of the Holy Spirit. This is God's

grace at its best! This is God's mercy at its best. Paul reminds us, as he does so many times in his letters, that we do not work for this, that we do not earn it, and that salvation is not given to us because we are so righteous and worthy. No! Once we accept with our hearts that Jesus went to the cross and took on every sin that we all have ever committed or will commit, then God's Holy Spirit pulls out the soap and shampoo and cleans us up until we are a new person. That is the holy shower of Jesus's sacrifice. If Jesus was willing to wash his disciple's dirty and smelly feet, then why won't He do the same thing for us? He will! Why? Because He loves us.

A friend of mine likes to say that when we die and stand before Jesus, Jesus is not going to say, "Don, what a wonderful resume you have. Look at all of your accomplishments. Man, you are at the top of your game. Come on in." I guess in some ways, that would be really good for a prideful, selfish person—which we all are—to receive such a compliment from Jesus Himself. That, however, is not how salvation works. Once again, we are not saved for the things done in this life. We are saved simply because of God's grace and mercy by sending His son to the cross so that our sins could be forgiven. Again, so long as we accept that with all of our hearts and minds and be willing to repent of our sins, then the bath is ready, the shower has been turned on. Get clean and be that new person in Christ!

Thought: Have you taken the divine shower yet? If yes, wasn't it just great! If not yet, get ready because it will be wonderful!

Let us pray: Dear Holy Lord, we belong to You today through the death and resurrection of Jesus. We pray that your will be done every moment of every day in our lives. May we continuously be filled by the renewing and cleansing power of Your Holy Spirit so that Jesus can live through us and in us. Amen.

FAITH AND WORKS

*What good is it, my brothers and sisters, if someone
claims to have faith but has no deeds? Can such faith
save them? Suppose a brother or a sister is without
clothes and daily food. If one of you says to them, "Go in
peace; keep warm and well fed," but does nothing about
their physical needs, what good is it? In the same way,
faith by itself, if not accompanied by action, is dead.*

—James 2:14–17 NIV

I WANT TO MAKE AN ANALOGY USING THE WORLD OF COLLEGE
football. Imagine there is a five-star recruit out of high school
who had phenomenal ability, and he accepted one of the many
offers from a particular college to play football. He arrived on
campus, and spring practice had begun. He often missed practice, he rarely was seen in the weight room, and his playbook
was on the shelf collecting dust. On the practice field, he rou-
tinely tuned out the coaches' directives and instructions, and he
developed a reputation for staying out late and not following
curfew rules. Needless to say, when the season started, he was
last on the depth chart for his position. Eventually, the college
pulled his scholarship, and he was cut from the team. He

thought his natural ability alone meant he could sail through the season, but he discovered that ability without practice and dedication is dead. Faith without works is dead.

I intentionally put this devotional from James immediately after the Day Twenty-Three devotional for a reason: so we could reconcile these two biblical principles. In yesterday's devotional, Paul reminds his readers that our salvation is not dependent on "righteous things we had done" or anything we will do. Salvation is dependent only on our acceptance of Christ as our Savior. So the emphasis by Paul is not on works. In today's devotion, however, James emphasizes that works are important. Do we have competing principles here? No! James is not saying that works provide us our faith. He is saying that our faith is evidenced by our works, our deeds, and our actions.

In general terms, here is what we do to show that our faith is real, authentic, and legitimate. We love life, we do good, and we seek peace. I love stories of simple acts of love and kindness, such as cutting a neighbor's yard when they are in the hospital or canceling an appointment in order to lend a listening ear to a friend's problem. We go out into the battlegrounds of life and help others in need. We take care of our families emotionally, physically, and spiritually. We promote honesty, compassion, and justice. If none of the above is in our "faith toolbox," then there needs to be a real re-examination of where our faith really is. So Paul says to accept Christ as Lord and Savior through faith, and James says to exhibit this faith through good works and actions. These good works do not need to be on the grand stage but just in the simple areas of life.

So let's go back to the college football player. His tremendous ability was of no worth or value since he did not work hard, practice hard, and study hard. His ability was simply dead. So it is with our faith. If we do not work our faith, show our faith, and use the gifts that God has given each one of us, then our faith is simply a fraud—a lifeless void hanging around our existence.

FAITH AND WORKS

Thought: How alive is your faith?

Let us pray: Our Father in Heaven, empower us with strong and everlasting faith in You, and help us show this faith by acts of love and grace for each other so that we can advance Your kingdom here on Earth. Show us how to bring You glory and honor by even simple acts of kindness and compassion. We praise Your holy name. Amen.

Day Twenty-Five

PRAYER

*Lord, the God of heaven, the great and awesome God,
who keeps his covenant of love with those who love him
and keep his commandments, let your ear be attentive
and your eyes open to hear the prayer your servant is
praying before you day and night for your servants, the
people of Israel. I confess the sins we Israelites, including
myself and my father's family, have committed against
you. We have acted very wickedly toward you. We have
not obeyed the commands, decrees and laws you gave
your servant Moses. Remember the instruction you gave
your servant Moses, saying, 'If you are unfaithful, I will
scatter you among the nations, but if you return to me
and obey my commands, then even if your exiled people
are at the farthest horizon, I will gather them from there
and bring them to the place I have chosen as a dwelling
for my Name.' They are your servants and your people,
whom you redeemed by your great strength and your
mighty hand. Lord, let your ear be attentive to the prayer
of this your servant and to the prayer of your servants
who delight in revering your name. Give your servant
success today by granting him favor in the presence of
this man.*

—Nehemiah 1:5–11 NIV

TODAY'S PASSAGE CONTAINS ONE OF THE GREAT PRAYERS FOUND IN
the Bible. Nehemiah is considered to be the last historian in the
Old Testament and also a cupbearer by trade. Nehemiah con-
fesses and intercedes before God. He acknowledges the greatness and love of God. Nehemiah prays with a wonderful sense
of humility.

I want to pull several verses from this prayer and see how
we today can identify with Nehemiah.

*Lord, the God of heaven, the great and awesome God, who keeps
his covenant of love with those who love him and keep his
commandments. (Verse 5)*

God is an awesome and loving God who keeps his promises.
We should always remain keenly aware of how awesome God
is and that He always keeps His promise that He loves his children. We should love Him back and do what He wants us to
do. But you know, even when we are not very loving and stray
from God's path, He still loves us, still provides for us, and is
there with open arms when we return to Him. He keeps His
promise that He will protect us and give us strength in times of
trouble. We have an awesome God who we can turn to when
we feel that there is no way out of the darkness we find ourselves in. We have an awesome God who gives us peace and
joy that simply gives us life to the full. These are great assurances for believers.

*I confess the sins we Israelites, including myself and my father's
family, have committed against you. (Verse 6b)*

We need to always recognize and confess our sinfulness. When
Nehemiah prayed this prayer, he was focusing on Israel's great
sin of idolatry. When you think of it, idolatry is a sin we all
commit each day. Look at the things we put ahead of God—our

jobs, our hobbies, and yes, even our wonderful families that we have. He simply wants to be first in our lives and in all that we do. He does not want to hold second place in our hearts.

Let your ear be attentive to the prayer of this your servant and to the prayer of your servants who delight in revering your name. (Verse 11)

God is always attentive to our prayers. We all experience the feeling that God does not hear us. We believe He is not listening because we have not received the response as quickly as we think we should or because He has not delivered up what we were praying for. But the fact remains that He does listen, and He does respond in His own way and in His own time. So remember, we need to pray to God and simply ask Him for patience so we can allow Him, as some say, to be God and let Him do His work. Let Him do His miracles. Let Him respond to our prayers in His perfect way.

As a slight deviation here, it is so hard for me to fathom just how many prayers go to God at the same time. I read somewhere that there may be 5–10 billion people in the world. Let's say that half of the total population pray to our God, and let's further say that 10% of those pray to God at the same time. That means that a quarter to a half a million people are praying to God at the very same time, that He is fielding every single prayer, and He has got each and every one down perfectly. Wow! We can be assured, however, even with all of those prayers, God cherishes our prayers very much.

I have read this prayer by Nehemiah many times, and what causes this prayer to stand out is that Nehemiah prays from the heart. While this prayer provides a lot of examples of good things we should pray about, the fact remains there is no set formula on how to pray. There is no set checklist on those things that must be in our prayers before God will accept them. No, what God wants is that our prayers be from the heart with the utmost sincerity and humility. That is what is so pleasing to our heavenly Father.

Thought: Do you struggle with praying? Do you feel like there are days when you do not feel like your prayers are right? I sure do!

Let us pray: Dear Our Awesome God, thank You for being such a loving and gracious God willing to accept us and love us even though we are full of sin and selfishness. Help us to practice patience, knowing that You hear every one of our prayers and that Your response to our prayers will be perfect and exactly what we need. Amen.

Day Twenty-Six

GOD HAS IT UNDER CONTROL

He says, "Be still, and know that I am God; I will be exalted among the nations, I will be exalted in the earth."

—Psalm 46:10 NIV

GOOD PARENTS ASSURE THEIR CHILDREN, ESPECIALLY YOUNG CHILdren, that they have matters under control. Parents do it either by words or by actions. Our children know that there will be food on the table, clothes on their backs, and a roof over their heads. Even when we parents experience some financial hardship or loss of a job, our children still know that they will be taken care of. I knew growing up my parents were not well-off by any means, but I knew they would find a way to provide for my brother and me. We knew that we would always get that one soft drink a week when my mother would take my brother and me to the store on Saturday for weekly grocery shopping and selection time for a Fanta grape drink or an Orange Crush.[1]

Just like our good parents, but much more so, our heavenly Father is dependable in that He will provide in every area of our lives. He tells us very plainly in today's scripture for us to be still. In other words, He says to slow down, don't be so anxious, and stop worrying and fretting. He then goes one step further and tells us why we should do this: because "I am God!" He says, "I am the creator and sustainer of all life. I created the heavens and the earth. I brought my most precious Son back to life." God says, "You think I cannot handle that problem of yours? Really?" What is our response? Our response is, "Remember He is God."

When the bank account gets a little low, remember He is God.

When the teenage daughter gets rebellious, remember He is God.

When retirement is coming soon, and you do not know what you are going to do, remember He is God.

When you get laid off from your job, remember He is God.

When your marriage begins taking some odd twists and turns, remember He is God.

When you get that bad test report from the doctor, remember He is God.

As hard as it is for us sometimes, we need to focus on the power and sovereignty of God and turn our worries, our problems, and our concerns over to Him.

Slow down, be still, take a breath, and then say, "Dear God, I turn this over to You for You to handle for me, please."

Thought: Is there a concern or problem in your life right now? Is it causing stress and anxiety? Are you trusting God as a good and dependable Father? Are you placing your trust in our loving Savior, Jesus? If not, then why not?

Let us pray: Lord Jesus, help me turn over every concern and worry that I have over to You knowing full well that there is nothing You cannot handle. Please give me that assurance when I need it. Help me to be still! Amen.

---

[1] I do not shop for soft drinks much these days. Do they still make a Fanta grape or an Orange Crush? Man, those were some good drinks back in the day!

Day Twenty-Seven

JESUS THE TEACHER

Jesus went throughout Galilee, teaching in their syna-gogues, proclaiming the good news of the kingdom, and healing every disease and sickness among the people.

—Matthew 4:23 NIV

MY DAUGHTER-IN-LAW, MANDY, WAS A FIRST-GRADE SCHOOL-teacher but now works in another area of education. Gayle was a long-time schoolteacher as well. They were both excellent teachers, and I am certain that many kids would not be where they are today if it had not been for the dedication and loyal teaching from Mandy and Gayle. The students are just better people because of these ladies.

Here are some statistics about teachers:[1]

- An average teacher affects over 3,000 students during their career

- 88% of people say a teacher had a significant positive impact on their life

- 75% of students say teachers are mentors and role models

- 79% of students say a teacher has encouraged them to follow their dreams

Jesus was also a great and wise teacher. There are many great attributes of Jesus, and certainly Savior is at the top of the list. Certainly, too, Jesus was sinless, holy, and absolutely perfect. But His teachings were flawless, so important, and such a large part of his ministry on Earth. Whether it was in front of large crowds or small, whether it was teaching a parable to his disciples, or whether it was performing some of his miracles, there was always a lesson to be learned. There was always some meaning to be gleaned from his instructions. Jesus always had a point to make. Just about any time He opened His mouth, there was teaching in the words. From teaching, the simple yet profound Beatitudes in the Sermon on the Mount[2] to the righteous display of anger when He cleared the temple of the merchants and money changers,[3] Jesus had something to say. Jesus again had a point to make.

Throughout the Gospels, Jesus taught us to love our neighbors as ourselves and to love our enemies. He taught us to seek forgiveness of our sins from our heavenly Father and to repent of our sins. Are we not better people because of the teachings of Jesus? Do we live more fulfilling lives because of what Jesus had to say? I believe so.

Picture this for me. Every time we open the Bible and turn to one of the Gospels, it is like we are sitting in a classroom and Jesus is the teacher. He says, "Boys and girls, turn to page … and the lesson for today is …." We are students of Jesus. As a teacher teaches students math and English, Jesus teaches us how to love and live life, to be good stewards of what we have been given, and to share with others the good news of forgiveness and salvation.

Thought: Jesus's classroom is a classroom we can be in every day of our lives.

Let us pray: Dear Jesus, thank You for being such a great teacher. Help me to be a better student. Help me to learn the lessons You want me to learn through Your study guide: the Bible. Amen.

---

[1] www.weareteachers.com "12 Powerful Statistics That Prove Why Teachers Matter," 5/15/19

[2] Matthew 5–7

[3] John 2

Day Twenty-Eight

WORRY

Then Jesus said to his disciples: "Therefore I tell you, do not worry about your life, what you will eat; or about your body, what you will wear. For life is more than food, and the body more than clothes. Consider the ravens: They do not sow or reap, they have no storeroom or barn; yet God feeds them. And how much more valuable you are than birds! Who of you by worrying can add a single hour to your life? Since you cannot do this very little thing, why do you worry about the rest? Consider how the wild flowers grow. They do not labor or spin. Yet I tell you, not even Solomon in all his splendor was dressed like one of these. If that is how God clothes the grass of the field, which is here today, and tomorrow is thrown into the fire, how much more will he clothe you — you of little faith! And do not set your heart on what you will eat or drink; do not worry about it. For the pagan world runs after all such things, and your Father knows that you need them. But seek his kingdom, and these things will be given to you as well. Do not be afraid, little flock, for your Father has been pleased to give you the kingdom."

—Luke 12:22–32 NIV

HAVE YOU EVER HEARD THE SAYING, "WORRY IS LIKE A ROCKING chair: it gives you something to do, but it gets you nowhere"? We have always heard that 85% of the things we worry about simply do not happen. There you go—the rocking chair.

Worry just ain't a good thing. Here is why:

- Medical research has shown that worry and stress break down our resistance to disease.

- Worry will just zap our strength. It will take enjoyment out of life. It will strangle our very being.

- Most importantly, worry causes us to lose our trust in our heavenly Father. We lose sight of the fact that He is always in control.

Jesus tells us that worry is not going to add one hour to our lives. Maybe Jesus should have gone on to say that worry can actually take an hour or two away from our lives!

Jesus tells us in John 16:33 that He gives us peace because He is mightier than this world. Remember, we have Jesus on our side—every hour, every day!

So what can we do about worry? What is the cure, doctor? I have some ideas.

1. Count your many blessings. When you feel that ting of anxiety coming over you, think of how God has blessed you. For me, it is my Lord and Savior, Jesus; my tremendous family; a great career; and that venison tenderloin stuffed with cream cheese and jalapeno peppers and wrapped in applewood bacon my son, Mike, recently put on the grill.[1] Every one of my blessings and every one of your blessings will put a smile on your face.

2. Pray. The great apostle Peter tells us in 1 Peter 5:7 to "Cast all of your cares upon Him for He cares about you." (NIV) We all have our favorite places to pray. My favorite place is in my car when I am traveling down the road, and I do not hold back in the tone or volume in my voice or in my mannerisms.[2] Prayer is the great equalizer to many things that ail us. To close on this point, Martin Luther said, "Pray and let God do the worrying."

3. Embrace the small moments in your life. Allow me to quote from author and pastor Craig Groeschel. He says, "The longer I live, the more I realize that our best life exists in embracing the small moments. If you look carefully, you might find your own special moment to grasp today. Seize it. Enjoy it. Embrace it. Thank God for it."[3] We have many small moments and blessings in our lives. I imagine more small ones than bigger ones. Our focus is now on the small moments and blessings and not on our worry about the problem or situation that we are in.

4. Recognize that we will always have trials and tribulations. God has never promised us a pain-free life. On the contrary, Jesus tells us that we will have trials. That is life in a fallen and sinful world. When we have a trial, a difficulty in life, we have the tools to combat it. We have a great and merciful God who we can be grateful to and seek His grace and mercy. We have a Savior in Jesus who we can find rest and peace. We have a Holy Spirit who gives us guidance and direction.

So, do we want worry, or do we want peace and that sustaining hope? I believe the choice is clear.

Thought: The next time you feel that grip of worry and fear come over you, count your many blessings and get on your knees and reach out to our Father in heaven.

Let us pray: Dear Lord, it is so reassuring that we have You and Your love. Never let us lose our trust in You, knowing in whatever situation we may find ourselves in that You are in control and that no problem, difficulty, or trial is too big for You. Amen.

---

[1] Oh, they were so good! I even took an extra cholesterol pill before I ate that day.

[2] Quite to the surprise sometimes of other travelers on the road.

[3] *Daily Power* devotional book, September 10th devotional

Day Twenty-Nine

WISDOM

*Blessed are those who find wisdom, those who gain un-
derstanding, for she is more profitable than silver and
yields better returns than gold. She is more precious than
rubies; nothing you desire can compare with her.*

—Proverbs 3:13–15 NIV

I HAVE A SMART FAMILY. MY WIFE, GAYLE, MY DAUGHTER,
Kathryn, and my daughter-in-law, Mandy, all have master's
degrees and beyond. My son, Mike, has a college degree and
has quite the unique ability to observe and soak in knowledge.
Kathryn was Phi Beta Kappa in college and is currently in man-
agement with her company. As I said in a prior devotional,
Mandy and Gayle were teachers and excellent at that. To round
us out, my grandson, Ford, is developmentally beyond his age,
according to his pediatrician. So there you have it—a lot of wisdom; therefore, a lot of knowledge and a lot of good ole' smarts.

We know that family wisdom is important, but we need to
step back a minute and look closer at what this scripture is really telling us. Certainly, if you pull up a dictionary, you will find
one definition for wisdom is knowledge, and that wisdom
equates to soundness of action or decision. Let's study this.

If you go to verse 21 in Proverbs 3 (NIV), it says this: "My son, do not let wisdom and understanding out of your sight, preserve sound judgment and discretion." Also, James 3:13 (NIV) says, "Who is wise and understanding among you? Let them show it by their good life, by deeds done in the humility that comes from wisdom."

So what is scripture trying to tell us about wisdom? Is it more than just knowing things? Is it about making good choices? It is about serving others. It is about living a life that is consumed with humility. It is always about seeking the will of God and doing what brings Him honor and glory. You can have all the degrees in the world plastered on the wall, the most prestigious of careers, and as much fame and recognition that one can handle, but God will not call you wise. What God wants is a humble servant who does the good things, the right things. He wants a follower who recognizes his shortcomings and his sinful ways. He wants a child who knows that his Father in heaven loves him, will always protect him, and will have perfect plans for his life. That, my friends, is wisdom! True wisdom!

Thought: Is wisdom important to you? If so, how do you apply it to your life?

Let us pray: Father God, help me first to understand and fully appreciate what true wisdom really is, and then help me to live a life that is truly wise and abundantly full of Your love and grace. Amen.

Day Thirty

ACCOUNTABILITY TO GOD

Now all has been heard; here is the conclusion of the matter: Fear God and keep his commandments, for this is the duty of all mankind. For God will bring every deed into judgment, including every hidden thing, whether it is good or evil.

—Ecclesiastes 12:13–14 NIV

THIS PASSAGE CONTAINS TWO KEY POINTS. FIRST OF ALL, WE ARE told to fear God and do as He commands. Maybe you already know that when scripture tells us to fear God, we are not being told to be afraid of him. Not at all! That is absolutely the last thing God wants us to do. What He wants of us is for us to revere Him, respect Him, and worship Him. We should be keenly aware of His power and might. So when we have this fear of Him, then the logical conclusion is that we should want to follow His commands. Godly fear is followed by a true desire to do everything that God expects of us.

Secondly, we are told that God's judgment will apply to everyone. Not just to a select group. Not to a certain number of people. No, every single member of all of humanity will be judged. Should this bring us comfort? I believe that it should. God does not play favorites. Think of some phrases and idioms that depict the idea of being treated the same. Here are some that come to my mind:

"I am going to feed everyone out of the same spoon."[1]
"They are all cut from the same cloth."
"That boss is a slave driver to all of his employees."
"He just follows the crowd."

I mention these phrases and idioms to make the simple point that in life, we want to be treated the same as others and do not like it if someone is treated better than us.

God, however, is going to take this to another level in that He is going to judge everyone the same. Next, non-believers (and some people say believers too) will stand before the Great White Throne of Judgment (according to Revelation 20) and believers before the Judgment Seat of Christ (according to 1 Corinthians 3 and 2 Corinthians 5). Judgment will be determined, and believers will receive rewards for how we have lived our lives. Either way, we will all be held accountable. At the end of the day, for each of us, accountability is going to be the divine process in how our Lord views and judges us. So let us each ask ourselves the following questions:

Do we earnestly try to follow God's commands?

Do we live as though we have made Jesus our Lord and Savior?

Do we live a life doing good with a heart of love and service?

I believe that we must ask ourselves these key questions every day of our lives. We must do a very thorough inward examination—a complete spiritual accounting—when we ask ourselves these questions. It goes without question what the answers should be!

Allow me to close this devotional with one more question. Do we believe that God is a God of wrath when He is judging sin? Now, I have tried to be as positive as can be throughout this devotional book in emphasizing how good and loving our Father in heaven is. He is without question! However, we cannot be led down the wrong path that just because God is good, then He will not exercise His wrath when necessary. God hates sin, as I have stated before, so much that His son went to the cross. He commands our obedience. So we need to live our lives fully aware, without blinders on, that when God judges, He will judge. I encourage you, and I encourage myself, to be accountable each day to live a life worthy of your (and mine) calling that you have received. (Ephesians 4:1)

Thought: Is accountability important to you? Do you reflect on how you live your life each day? Do you strive to love the Lord with all your heart, treat others with respect and humility, and serve the Lord keeping all of his commands?

Let us pray: Dear Lord, we praise Your name, for You are an awesome God. You are a God of love but also a God of judgment who demands our obedience. We are sinful and so unworthy of Your grace and mercy. We when stray, bring us back into Your fold, reminding us that we will be held accountable for everything we have done in this life. Amen.

---

[1] Whoever came up with this one probably did not think much about cleanliness and the spread of germs!

Day Thirty-One

HEAVEN

After this I looked, and there before me was a great multitude that no one could count, from every nation, tribe, people and language, standing before the throne and before the Lamb. They were wearing white robes and were holding palm branches in their hands. And they cried out in a loud voice: "Salvation belongs to our God, who sits on the throne, and to the Lamb."

—Revelation 7:9–10 NIV

Then I saw "a new heaven and a new earth," for the first heaven and the first earth had passed away, and there was no longer any sea. I saw the Holy City, the new Jerusalem, coming down out of heaven from God, prepared as a bride beautifully dressed for her husband. And I heard a loud voice from the throne saying, "Look! God's dwelling place is now among the people, and he will dwell with them. They will be his people, and God himself will be with them and be their God. 'He will wipe every tear from their eyes. There will be no more death' or mourning or crying or pain, for the old order of things has passed away." He who is seated on the throne said, "I am making everything new!"

—Revelation 21:1–5a NIV

AS I ASKED PREVIOUSLY, HAVE YOU EVER WISHED THAT GOD would give us just a little more of what heaven is like? A few more details would be nice. A few more descriptions. Maybe a picture or two. Yeah, all of that would be nice, but then if we knew more, maybe a lot more, then it would take the "faith element " out of the equation. Or, if we knew more, our little finite minds may simply be blown away literally!

Jesus tells us in Chapter 14 of John, and I am paraphrasing here: "Hey, do not be worried or troubled about heaven. I've got this. I am going ahead of you and making sure that everything is going to be just perfect for you. Just wait and see." (verses 1–2) If we put our trust in Jesus as our Lord and Savior, then why can't we just trust Him that heaven is going to be a really good place? Trust is the key.

Secondly, we know from our two readings today that there is the initial heaven, and then there will be a second heaven when heaven and earth come together. Regardless of why that is going to be, we do know that there are going to be a lot of people praising God and worshipping Him. Why? I believe it is because there will be no more death, pain, tears, and anything negative that we experience here on earth. Admittedly, I have a great life. Great family and friends, great job, and so many blessings that I cannot begin to count. As great as life is, we still experience turmoil, disease, trials, and devastating tragedies. So, the logical conclusion must be heaven is a place with unsurpassed peace and joy, and on top of that, there is nothing bad that will ever go on there. I do not think it takes a rocket scientist to figure out what awaits us.

HEAVEN

The apostle Paul tells us we must live as "citizens of heaven." (Philippians 3:20) That is absolutely right. We must live life with at least one eye and one ear pointed towards heaven. Spending eternity with our heavenly Father and our Savior Jesus is the end goal for all of us. The reason I ended this book with this devotional from Revelation is that heaven is the culmination of everything we do here on this earth as believers. Living on this earth is that small dash between the date of our birth and the date of our death. How we live and what we believe will determine if we receive the grandest prize ever, and that is simply living with and worshiping our Lord in heaven. It is going to be so sweet and perfect. Add in our family and friends who have gone before us, and that makes it much sweeter.

Thought: How much do you think about heaven? Do you think about who you will see there or what you will do in heaven? Do you think about the eternal aspect of heaven or what heaven will actually look like? Or do you accept that heaven is going to be absolutely wonderful, and you are satisfied with that?

Let us pray: Oh, Holy Lord, fill our hearts and minds with thoughts of heaven and with thoughts of spending eternity with You. Please do not allow us to be preoccupied with thoughts of not knowing a lot about Your heavenly home. Please keep us content with what You have told us and give us that sense of excitement of what You have planned for us and for what is yet to come. Thank you! Amen.